For

With Love

Compiled by
Evelyn L. Beilenson

PETER PAUPER PRESS, INC.
WHITE PLAINS · NEW YORK

*Thanks to Laura Kuczma for
her editorial assistance*

For Helen and Peter

Peter Pauper Press, Inc.
202 Mamaroneck Avenue
White Plains, NY 10601
ISBN 0-88088-735-4
Printed in Hong Kong
12 11 10 9 8 7

...WITH LOVE

At the touch of love every one
becomes a poet.

Plato

Love may not make the world
go round, but I must admit
that it makes the ride
worthwhile.

Sean Connery

The truth [is] that there is
only one terminal dignity—
love. And the story of a love is
not important—what is
important is that one is
capable of love. It is perhaps
the only glimpse we are
permitted of eternity.

Helen Hayes

Love, you know, seeks to make
happy rather than to be happy.

Ralph Connor

Love is always patient and
kind; it is never jealous; love is
never boastful or conceited; it
is never rude or selfish; it does
not take offense, and is not
resentful. Love takes no
pleasure in other people's sins
but delights in the truth; it is
always ready to excuse, to
trust, to hope, and to endure
whatever comes.

Love does not come to an
end.

I Corinthians 13: 4-8
Jerusalem Bible

How absurd and delicious it is
to be in love with somebody
younger than yourself.
Everybody should try it.

Barbara Pym

Love makes the time pass.
Time makes love pass.

French Proverb

Men always want to be a woman's first love—women like to be a man's last romance.

Oscar Wilde

Marrying a man is like buying something you've been admiring for a long time in a shop window. You may love it when you get it home, but it doesn't always go with everything else in the house.

Jean Kerr

Love doesn't grow on trees
like apples in Eden—it's
something you have to make.
And you must use your
imagination too.

Joyce Cary

Don't smother each other. No
one can grow in shade.

Leo F. Buscaglia

Girls we love for what they are; young men for what they promise to be.

Johann Wolfgang von Goethe

The heart that loves is always young.

Greek Proverb

Love is I know not what, which
comes from I know not where
and which finishes I know not
how.

Scudéry

The more you judge, the less
you love.

Honoré de Balzac

Who travels for love finds a
thousand miles not longer
than one.

Japanese Proverb

No one perfectly loves God
who does not perfectly love
some of his creatures.

Marguerite de Valois

Escape me?
Never—
Beloved!
While I am I, and you are you,
  So long as the world
    contains us both,
  Me the loving and you
    the loth,
While the one eludes, must
the other pursue.

Robert Browning

Love tells us many things that are not so.

Ukrainian Proverb

Who ever loved, that loved not at first sight?

Christopher Marlowe

But, O Sarah! If the dead can come back to this earth and flit unseen around those they loved, I shall always be near you; in the gladdest days and in the darkest nights . . . *always, always,* and if there be a soft breeze upon your cheek, it shall be my breath, as the cool air fans your throbbing temple, it shall be my spirit passing by. Sarah, do not mourn me dead: think I am gone and wait for me, for we shall meet again.

Major Sullivan Ballou,
Union Army,
from a letter to his wife

The love we give away is the
only love we keep.
Elbert Hubbard

No one has ever loved anyone
the way everyone wants to be
loved.
Mignon McLaughlin

Many waters cannot quench love, neither can the floods drown it.

Song of Solomon 8: 7

You don't suffer, kill yourself and take the risks I take just for money. I love bike racing.

Greg LeMond

When you love someone all
your saved up wishes start
coming out.

Elizabeth Bowen

Ah, Celeste, my pretty jewel, I
love you as a pig loves the
mud!

Creole Proverb

All married couples should
learn the art of battle as they
should learn the art of making
love. Good battle is objective
and honest—never vicious or
cruel. Good battle is healthy
and constructive, and brings
to a marriage the principles of
equal partnership.

Ann Landers

Love looks through a telescope;
envy, through a microscope.

Josh Billings

Can one ever remember love?
It's like trying to summon
up the smell of roses in a cellar.
You might see a rose, but
never the perfume.

Arthur Miller

Nobody can have the soul of
me. My mother has had it, and
nobody can have it again.
Nobody can come into my very
self again, and breathe me like
an atmosphere.

D. H. Lawrence

How do you know love is gone? If you said that you would be there at seven and you get there by nine, and he or she has not called the police yet,—it's gone.

Marlene Dietrich

Love is like the measles; we all have to go through it.

Jerome K. Jerome

Courtship consists in a number of quiet attentions, not so pointed as to alarm, nor so vague as not to be understood.

Laurence Sterne

The ability to make love frivolously is the thing which distinguishes human beings from the beasts.

Heywood Broun

A lover always thinks of his mistress first and himself second; with a husband it runs the other way.

Honoré de Balzac

One advantage of marriage, it seems to me, is that when you fall out of love with him, or he falls out of love with you, it keeps you together until you maybe fall in again.

Judith Viorst

Kindness and intelligence
don't always deliver us from
the pitfalls and traps: there are
always failures of love, of will,
of imagination. There is no
way to take the danger out of
human relationships.

Barbara Grizzuti Harrison

There are more people who
wish to be loved than there are
who are willing to love.

Sébastien Roch
Nicolas Chamfort

Love is supposed to start with
bells ringing and go downhill
from there. But it was the
opposite for me. There's an
intense connection between
us, and as we stayed together,
the bells rang louder.

Lisa Niemi

Love keeps the cold out better
than a cloak.

Henry Wadsworth Longfellow

Gather ye rosebuds while
ye may,
    Old Time is still a-flying;
And this same flower that
smiles today
    Tomorrow will be dying.
                    Robert Herrick

Follow love and it will flee,
Flee love and it will follow
thee.

                    John Gay

Love does not dominate; it cultivates.

Johann Wolfgang von Goethe

So dear I love him that with him all deaths I could endure, without him live no life.

John Milton

If you want to be loved, be lovable.

Ovid

I have found it impossible to carry the heavy burden of responsibility and to discharge my duties as king as I would wish to do without the help and support of the woman I love.

Edward, Duke of Windsor

To be in love is merely to be in
a state of perceptual
anesthesia—to mistake an
ordinary young woman for
a goddess.

H. L. Mencken

Hell's afloat in lovers' tears.
Attributed to *Dorothy Parker*

A life without love in it is like
a heap of ashes upon a
deserted hearth—with the fire
dead, the laughter stilled, and
the light extinguished.

Frank P. Tebbetts

Don't let love interfere with
your appetite. It never does
with mine.

Anthony Trollope

At a cocktail party the other night I looked across a crowded room and was taken by a stranger, in half profile, a handsome, terribly young-looking man with a halo of backlighted curls. And then he turned and I realized that it was the stranger I am married to, the beneficiary on my insurance policy, the sport jacket, the love of my life.

Anna Quindlen

Love and eggs are best when
they are fresh.

Russian Proverb

There is nothing holier, in this
life of ours, than the first
consciousness of love—the
first fluttering of its silken
wings.

Henry Wadsworth Longfellow

Marriages are made in heaven
and consummated on earth.
French Proverb

There is no fear in love; but
perfect love drives out fear.
I John 4:18

To love is to find pleasure in
the happiness of the person
loved.

*Baron Gottfried Wilhelm
von Leibnitz*

A woman either loves or hates;
she knows no medium.

Publilius

Love is the whole history of a woman's life, it is but an episode in a man's.

Madame de Staël

Women love always: when earth slips from them, they take refuge in heaven.

George Sand

Marriage resembles a pair of
shears, so joined that they
cannot be separated, often
moving in opposite directions,
yet always punishing anyone
who comes between them.

Sydney Smith

Take away love, and our earth
is a tomb.

Robert Browning

The honey is sweet, but the
bee has a sting.

Benjamin Franklin

Why did she love him?
Curious fool—be still—
Is human love the growth of
human will?

Lord Byron

At the end of what is called the "sexual life" the only love which has lasted is the love which has everything, every disappointment, every failure and every betrayal, which has accepted even the sad fact that in the end there is no desire so deep as the simple desire for companionship.

Graham Greene

A man is not where he lives, but where he loves.

Latin Proverb

Jealousy comes more from
self-love than from true love.
Duc de La Rochefoucauld

Whither thou goest, I will go;
and where thou lodgest, I will
lodge; thy people shall be my
people, and thy God my God.
Ruth 1:16

I see when men love women
They give them but a little
    of their lives
But women when they love
    give everything.
                    Oscar Wilde

Where there is love there is
no sin.
                    Montenegrin

I've never been in love. I've
always been a lawyer.

Unknown

A woman can be anything the
man who loves her would have
her be.

James Barrie

True love is like a psychic experience. Everyone tells ghost stories, but few have ever seen a ghost.

Duc de La Rochefoucauld

Love is much nicer to be in than an automobile accident, a tight girdle, a higher tax bracket, or a holding pattern over Philadelphia.

Judith Viorst

The first duty of love is to listen.

Paul Tillich

After the verb "to love," "to help" is the most beautiful verb in the world!

Baroness Bertha von Suttner

Love comforteth like sunshine
after rain.

William Shakespeare

Paradise was made for tender
hearts; hell, for loveless hearts.

Voltaire

A woman knows the face of
the man she loves as a sailor
knows the open sea.

Honoré de Balzac

He who is not impatient is not
in love.

Italian Proverb

Love is the master key that
opens the gates of happiness.
Oliver Wendell Holmes

No cord or cable can draw so
forcibly, or bind so fast, as
love can do with a single
thread.

Robert Burton

Love is like quicksilver in the
hand. Leave the fingers open
and it stays. Clutch it, and it
darts away.

Dorothy Parker

Don't brood. Get on with
living and loving. You don't
have forever.

Leo F. Buscaglia

Love is like linen: often
changed, the sweeter.

Love can never more grow old,
Locks may lose their brown
    and gold,
Cheeks may fade and hollow
    grow,
But the hearts that love
    will know
Never winter's frost and chill,
Summer's warmth is in them
    still.

Eben Eugene Rexford

No more we meet in yonder
    bowers;
Absence has made me prone
    to roving;
But older, firmer hearts
    than ours,
Have found monotony in
    loving.

Lord Byron

I just want to get a Ph.D. in
love.

Barbara De Angelis

When women love us, they
forgive us everything, even our
crimes; when they do not love
us, they give us credit for
nothing, not even our virtues.

Honoré de Balzac

The surest way to hit a
woman's heart is to take aim
kneeling.

Douglas Jerrold

The whisper of a pretty girl
can be heard further than the
roar of a lion.

Arab Proverb

You can't force anyone to love
you or to lend you money.

Jewish Proverb

When we are in love we seem
to ourselves quite different
from what we were before.
Blaise Pascal

To love oneself is the beginning
of a lifelong romance.
Oscar Wilde

Who loves, raves.

Lord Byron

It is easier to be a lover than a husband for the simple reason that it is more difficult to be witty every day than to say pretty things from time to time.

Honoré de Balzac

He is not a lover who does not
love forever.

Euripides

He that hath love in his breast
hath spurs in his sides.

Herbert

Love is a canvas pattern
furnished by Nature, and
embroidered by imagination.

Voltaire

Love is the only sane and
satisfactory answer to the
problem of human existence.

Erich Fromm

It is never too late to fall in love.

Sandy Wilson

Love is the child of illusion
and the parent of disillusion.

Miguel de Unamuno

A successful marriage requires
falling in love many times,
always with the same person.
Mignon McLaughlin

A heart in love with beauty
never grows old.
Ancient Turkish Proverb

Many a man in love with a
dimple makes the mistake of
marrying the whole girl.
                    Stephen Leacock

It is difficult to know at what
moment love begins; it is less
difficult to know that it has
begun.

Henry Wadsworth Longfellow

Stay me with flagons, comfort
me with apples: for I am sick
of love.

Song of Solomon 2:5

God is love, but get it
in writing.

Gypsy Rose Lee

Love thou the rose, yet leave it on its stem.

Edward Robert Bulwer-Lytton

One should always be in love. That is the reason one should never marry.

Oscar Wilde

It is the woman who chooses
the man who will choose her.
Paul Geraldy

Love is the only weapon we
need.
Rev. H. R. L. Sheppard

Love is the delusion that one
woman differs from another.

H. L. Mencken

To witness two lovers is a
spectacle for the gods.

Johann Wolfgang von Goethe

Respect is love in plain
clothes.

Frankie Byrne

Nobody loves a woman because
she is handsome or ugly,
stupid or intelligent. We love
because we love.

Honoré de Balzac

Infatuation is when you think that he's as sexy as Robert Redford, as smart as Henry Kissinger, as noble as Ralph Nader, as funny as Woody Allen, and as athletic as Jimmy Connors. Love is when you realize that he's as sexy as Woody Allen, as smart as Jimmy Connors, as funny as Ralph Nader, as athletic as Henry Kissinger and nothing like Robert Redford—but you'll take him anyway.

Judith Viorst

Sex is a momentary itch,
Love never lets you go.

Kingsley Amis

I know nothing about platonic
love except that it is not to be
found in the works of Plato.

Edgar Jepson

'Tis better to have loved and
   lost
Than never to have loved
   at all.

        Alfred, Lord Tennyson

Among those whom I like or
admire, I can find no common
denominator, but among those
whom I love, I can: all of them
make me laugh.

        W. H. Auden

Thou art my own, my darling,
   and my wife;
And when we pass into
   another life,
Still thou art mine. All
   this which now we see
Is but the childhood
   of Eternity.
              Arthur Joseph Munby

Love is love's reward.
              John Dryden

I know the difference now
between dedication and
infatuation. That doesn't mean
I don't still get an enormous
kick out of infatuation: the
exciting ephemera, the punch
in the stomach, the adrenaline
to the heart.

Anna Quindlen

He who marries for love
without money has good
nights and sorry days.

Jesus said love one another.
He didn't say love the whole
world.

Mother Teresa

Just a wee cot—the crickets
chirr—love and the smiling
face of her.

James Whitcomb Riley

Love and tooth-ache have
many cures, but none infallible,
except possession and
dispossession.
                    Benjamin Franklin

The mind has a thousand eyes,
    And the heart but one;
Yet the light of a whole
life dies
    When love is done.
        Francis William Bourdillon